FIRST EXPERIENCES

FIONA'S FIRST DAY OF SCHOOL

by Mari Schuh
illustrated by Daniela Massironi

GRASSHOPPER

Tools for Parents & Teachers

Grasshopper Books enhance imagination and introduce the earliest readers to fiction with fun storylines and illustrations. The easy-to-read text supports early reading experiences with repetitive sentence patterns and sight words.

Before Reading

- Look at the cover illustration. What do readers see? What do they think the book will be about?

- Look at the picture glossary together. Sound out the words. Ask readers to identify the first letter of each vocabulary word.

Read the Book

- "Walk" through the book, reading to or along with the reader. Point to the illustrations as you read.

After Reading

- Review the picture glossary again. Ask readers to locate the words in the text.

- Ask the reader: How does Fiona feel before her first day of school? How does she feel after? How do you know?

Grasshopper Books are published by Jump!
5357 Penn Avenue South
Minneapolis, MN 55419
www.jumplibrary.com

Copyright © 2023 Jump! International copyright reserved in all countries. No part of this book may be reproduced in any form without written permission from the publisher.

Library of Congress Cataloging-in-Publication Data

Names: Schuh, Mari C., 1975- author.
Massironi, Daniela, illustrator.
Title: Fiona's first day of school / by Mari Schuh; illustrated by Daniela Massironi.
Description: Minneapolis, MN: Jump!, Inc., [2023]
Series: First experiences
Audience: Ages 4-7.
Identifiers: LCCN 2021059773 (print)
LCCN 2021059774 (ebook)
ISBN 9781636909271 (hardcover)
ISBN 9781636909288 (paperback)
ISBN 9781636909295 (ebook)
Subjects: LCSH: Readers (Primary)
First day of school–Juvenile fiction.
LCGFT: Readers (Publications)
Classification: LCC PE1119.2 .S374 2023 (print)
LCC PE1119.2 (ebook)
DDC 428.6/2–dc23/eng/20211216
LC record available at https://lccn.loc.gov/2021059773
LC ebook record available at https://lccn.loc.gov/2021059774

Editor: Jenna Gleisner
Direction and Layout: Anna Peterson
Illustrator: Daniela Massironi

Printed in the United States of America at Corporate Graphics in North Mankato, Minnesota.

Table of Contents

New Places and Faces	4
Let's Review!	16
Picture Glossary	16

New Places and Faces

"Are you excited for your first day of school, Fiona?" Dad asks.

"I'm nervous," I say. "I won't know anyone. And what if I miss you?"

"Your brother will be in the same building," Dad says. "Take this photo of us with you. Look at it when you miss me."

Dad walks me to my classroom.

I see my teacher! I met her this summer.

"Have fun, Fiona! I will pick you up after school," Dad says.

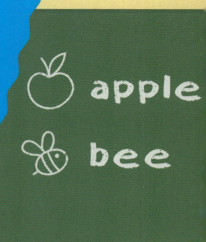

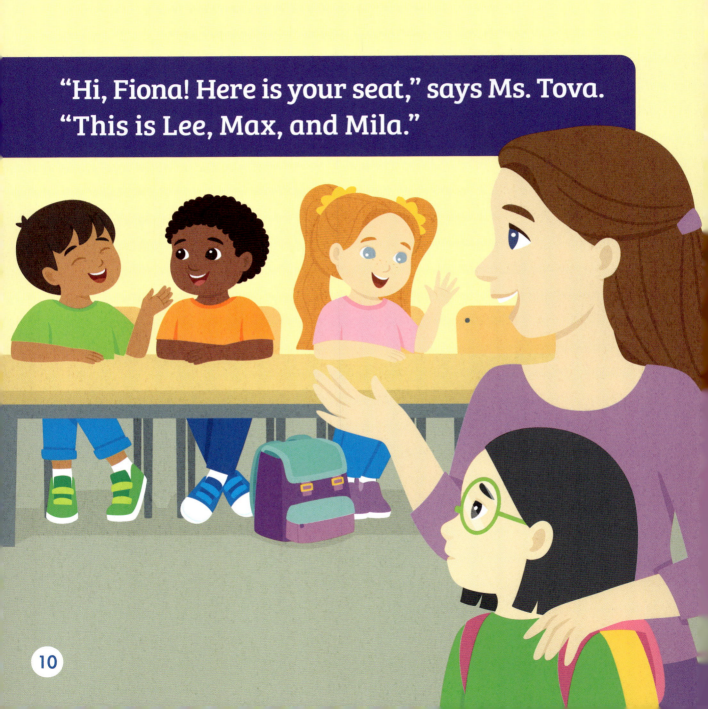
"Hi, Fiona! Here is your seat," says Ms. Tova. "This is Lee, Max, and Mila."

At lunch, I don't know where to sit.

"We can sit together!" Mila says.

I am happy.

I didn't want to sit alone.

After school, Dad picks me up.

"How was your first day?" he asks.

"It was fun! I made a new friend!" I say.

Let's Review!

What makes Fiona feel better on her first day of school?

A. She brings a photo of her family.   **B.** She makes a new friend.
C. She wins tag at recess.   **D.** She brings her favorite stuffed animal.

Picture Glossary

backpack
A bag that you carry on your back, which holds your supplies.

excited
Eager and interested.

nervous
Anxious or worried about something.

teacher
A person who teaches and helps people learn.